A Wilderness of Monkeys

Aphorisms & Divagations

by
Page Nelson

Edited and with an Introduction
by
William Ruminant

Another
Sparrow
Press

© Copyright 2012 Page Nelson

Published by Another Sparrow Press, the publishing branch
for fine arts and the humanities
of Passerine Inc., a global multi-media entertainment provider

Page Nelson asserts his moral right not to be identified as the author of this work; any reproduction, transmission, broadcast or rebroadcast in any form or by any means, digital, mechanical, pastoral-mechanical including photocopy, recording or storage by any retrieval system without prior permission of the publisher is permitted.

Chinese edition forthcoming as: 從西部太陽的前光芒
[Hong Kong, Green Chamber Press, 2012]
All rights reserved.

ISBN: 978-0615582740

Cataloging-at-Publication Data
Nelson, Page, 1952-
A Wilderness of Monkeys: Aphorisms & Divagations / by Page Nelson.
   1. Aphorisms and apothegms.   I. Ruminant, William.   II. Title
PN6271.N44 2012   2012
                          CAP/NOTCIP

Book design by Jo-Anne Rosen, Petaluma, California

Cover art: Monkeys by Mori Sosen, with permission, the British Museum (© Trustees of the British Museum)

Back cover: Apes in a persimmon-tree by Mori Sosen (detail)

Sparrow. Beauty of the sparrow's shape and flight — Activity and life. Not to go too much into the abstract – the opposite; chaffinch and sparrow understood — Nearer conveying and near to the real truth than the most polished abstract, however guarded.

from the Notebooks of Richard Jefferies

Introduction

Historically, aphoristic utterances trail the major work; they are sparks from the great fire; we think of Wilde, Kafka, the collected wit and wisdom of almost anyone in the canon. Even as natural an aphorist as Nietzsche had first composed lengthy monographs before being compelled in mid-career into briefer forms that still functioned as an extended figure of his argument and prose.

Our author attempts to short circuit the creative process, saving us and himself, the heavy lifting of a magnum opus, cutting to the chase via concise pronouncements. We may suspect that it isn't quite that easy, that the freestanding aphorism, lacking the gravity and controlment of a major star, is less illuminating meteor than drifting mote of dust.

Nelson's bits are related by mood and method to that most typical American genre, the short, "free verse" lyric that refusing meter and rhyme, seeks conviction via imagistic and congestive intensity. (That poetry is one of his constant subjects or topical victims would lead one to suspect he was an attempting practitioner, though no such efforts survive.) To his credit, he doesn't segregate himself from "the wilderness of monkeys," his borrowed (from Shakespeare) and dismissively collective noun for humanity, demonstrating in his work that we are more likely to jabber Truth than Beauty and neither reliably.

Alternate titles for this collection, as can be see from notebooks deposited in The Small Special Collections Department at the University of Virginia, were "Shards" and "Temporary Arrangements" rejected, he says, because the former implies a tikunic restoration or reassembly and the latter, that there is some arrangement other than the "temporary."

Such a critical position, a via negativa (self-consciously indebted to Adorno) must have made him suspect (and ultimately endorse) the episodic program of a work lacking organic form when that is a structural virtue of the merest American poem he purports to scorn.

The book was composed over a relatively short period, from early winter 2010, to late spring 2011, roughly Thanksgiving to Easter. Everything suggests is the dented fruit of a lifetime of reading, a proportionately thin distilment reflecting a long, slim life. If the virtue of its almost commendable range of reference is vitiated by his "posts" staking out not a position but in conjuring, vaguely, a void, the amplitudious reader may yet find gratification not in what Wilderness of Monkeys says but in what it doesn't; value it not for what it is but for what it so distinctly isn't.

William Ruminant
Dept. of Comparative Literature
Edmister University
Verver, Indiana

Editor's Note

The manuscript of *A Wilderness of Monkeys* is contained in three 6 by 4 inch black leather bound notebooks, designated A, B and C, with B, the graph square papered one composing three quarters of the book's final content. The text was subsequently typed into Word on a 2005 model ThinkCentre IBM computer. Copies of the word processed document were printed weekly, edited and amended in hand by both addition and subtraction and these revisions then retyped in the existing file. Transfer to print was effected by mean of a 3 x 5 inch floppy disc, as the author lacked a home printer. None of these "working" documents survive. The disc, archived in the Founder's Papers at the William Ruminent Center for Bibliographical Studies at Edmister University's Wilbur Memorial Library, constitutes the copy text in a bowersonian sense, though the notebooks have been consulted as needed.

Editorial intervention has been minimal aside from correction of misspellings; every effort has been made to identify and preserve intentional neologisms. Grammatical mistakes have been selectively retained as deliberate or characteristic of the author's "style." The propositions have been numbered to permit coherence indexing. The endnotes, inappropriately daggered not numbered, are the author's. In a few instances where it is deemed likely the author's obliquely humorous intentions may be mistaken for serious statement, the editor has imposed a terminal indicator of [h?].

W.R.

A Wilderness
of Monkeys

[1] Demoralized population, bankrupt finances, an effective military good for victories in a few final wars, decline not yet defined; 17th century Spain, 21st century America.

[2] *Decline of America II.* Horseracing, a spectator sport the enjoyment of which increased with every stake of intelligence (handicapping) lapped in popular appeal by NASCAR, a circular track of sound and fury signifying nothing. *Contrapuntal.* Auto racing being more humane than gladiator bouts, bear baiting, heretic burning, witch hunting, ritual sacrifice (Aztecs), public torture (China), bullfighting and bare knuckle boxing, its fans are among the most progressive specimens of humanity.

[3] Walking down any American sidewalk, one notices the concrete is spectacled with black dots, thousands of pressed globs, more than the city's population. America, land of the free, home of the gum droppers. (Since carelessness is seldom cruel but cruelty is always careless, the Singaporean police, writing tickets for gum-dropping, are doing their little bit for benevolence.)

[4] Great advantage of the book; "connected" only to itself, it reaches out with the self procession of a thinking mind.

[5] France. What nation has done more for the life of Art or for the art of Life?†

[6] I miss the naïve pollsters in the 1960s who would stop my mother on the street, assume she was Christian and ask, "what is your denomination?" I would love to answer "Dreyfusian," telling them the story of the noble military Jew, mocked in multiple trials, degraded before the mob, tortured for five years on Devil's Island who yet could say "I bear no one any hatred."

[7] Were I to found a religion, it would be upon a single tenet: "Be kind to animals, including human ones." Of course, subsequent disciples would kill, hashing out the doctrinal details.

[8] Certain juxtapositions of cultural complexity, people conversant, say, with Hegel (once as common as reading music) stimulate adjacent sophistications, the novels of Henry James. Eliminating any region of cultural competence impoverishes the future. Innovation doesn't just fly into the Petri dish; it flourishes in an over rich culture.

[9] Importance of squirrels and sparrows: in cities, the most common, natural critics of our human order. That for habitat they've come to rely on it demonstrates their qualification in the matter.

[10] For all the cultural apologetics, the great miracle: Sophocles and Shakespeare as *popular* entertainments.

[11] Tibetan Buddhism. Admirable except for the oddity of karma and vowed obedience to the guru which demands the relinquishing of the greatest treasure, our critical capacity. So valuable, is it not most proper for sacrifice? For what is it protecting – a petty Ego, the illusion of an essential Self? Yet gurus have been known (shown) to be no more than little selves. One should not give up anything so practical as our questioning acuity for the elegance of an argument or easement of an answer.†

[12] Faced with dissolution, even Buddhists desire continuance, hence reincarnation. Philosophers see how every good – animal life, human culture even great creating Nature disappears down the funnel of annihilation. Nothing lasts. Unless God is a kind of hard drive, desirously retentive of the Good, preserving us in paradise since most of us contain atoms of goodness. And if you believe that, what exactly you would not believe?

[13] While not personally anti-Semitic, Nietzsche when he sent the Superman out on his mission of demolishing bourgeois Judeo-Christian morality, whom did he suppose would be ultimate victims – parish priests, government clerks or the usual Jews?

[14] Being rather slow on the uptake, it took me a while to recognize that the best part of most books is the epigram introducing a chapter.

[15] Among Americans, only Southerners whose ancestors gave blood and treasure to the uttermost for one of the worst causes conceivable, a weak North American splinter state, based on slavery and subjected to European power, understand in their marrow irony.

[16] The Protestant Reformation. Odd that a movement so convinced of human depravity that redemption was by grace alone, liberated human potential. Clear the decks of popes, priests, entire libraries of theology and canon law; all that's needed is the Book read in the vernacular, subjected to the most local and personal interpretation. "Interpret" means "live free." For all its baggage, "Ein Feste Burg" is an anthem of liberty.

[17] If 6000 American poets boarded one of those garish, top heavy, casino-type cruise ships and never returned, what effect would this have on literary culture? A deterioration? A renewal? No effect whatsoever?

[18] In lyric poetry what matters is the achievement of a distinctive "tone," Keats must sound like Keats. To call this "music" misrepresents the topical/conceptual content, which, admittedly, is the least of it.

[19] Venice. You know the story – the UFO aliens lose patience (or complete their research project) and decide to rid the planet of its most pestilential species. Then one contrarian voice says – "there is Venice," that surpassingly human, all too human place and the ETs hesitate because humanity intensified to the Venetian degree is uncanny.†

[20] Best argument against extra terrestrials visiting the earth: why on earth would they care?

[21] Address to the 24th Regiment of Foot, before Iswandalana and Rorke's Drift.

> "Over the next 3 days, you will fight two terrible battles. Half will be killed, the rest wounded. But victory will result in sixty years of crown control and introduction of the rail road. Now march on."

[22] Empires are Kitsch.

[23] We perceive only 2% of the electromagnetic spectrum. Which leaves wide scope for "more in heaven and earth than dreamt of in your philosophy" or science.

> "Look how the floor of heaven
> Is thick inlaid with pattens of bright gold.
> There's not the smallest orb which thou beholdest
> But in his motion like an angel sings
> Still quiring to the young-eyed cherubims;
> Such harmony is in immortal souls
> But, whilst in this muddy vesture of decay
> Doth grossly close in it, we cannot hear it."
>
> (*The Merchant of Venice,* V.i)

[24] *Strange physics.* Iris Murdoch has it right (The Bell), the great thing about great art, greater than its vision or technique, is its inexhaustible generosity.

[25] After 21 years, the old cat is ailing. It had a good life, food, warmth, interest, love. Now it wails half-hourly in pain. It will have to be put down, one last trip to the kindly vet with her silver needle. One hates this irreversibility, the absolute loss, in a city not even a body left for consolation. Animals, that need no redemption, cannot be exempted from our conceits of resurrection.

[26] Rilke's lament for dogs: "these creatures we have helped up to a soul for which there is no heaven." No heaven for dogs, none for humans. You must refuse it (the final test of merit, Yudishthira's). Fortunately, it won't come to that.

[27] A very rich acquaintance has died. Today, all his wealth won't purchase another minute of life. Our fortunes are reversed. I live, I breathe.

[28] N*otes on architecture*. If architecture at its best is frozen music (and some modern buildings are good static jazz), go to any modern city and what you see is frozen noise, the skyline looking like the display of a digital sound meter.

Turn of the last century (2000/2001) architecture: beautiful prisons, penitential museums, the aesthetic stage of storage.

City: a moral theatre where the script, Art, is written after the fact, a civitas of sound and fury signifying something. Only culture distinguishes "urbs" from hive, being from bee.

Brutalistic buildings are "classics" because like the bunkers, flak towers, and submarine pens that inspired them, they have aesthetic endurance and never look any worse.

Since for architects, space is time, it's surprising so few buildings embody variant tempi given the exempla of cathedrals' centuries-span heterogeneity or the fast-slow detailing of a style many mistake as the most in one moment, Art Nouveau.

[29] Never having known a "normal" family life, I idealize it, observing in some families responsibility towards one's mate and responsibility for the children, behaviors evidencing self-sacrifice and love. What major philosopher of the last two centuries has led such a life? It's all very well to say they are progenitors of ideas, not brats. These are people you wouldn't trust to baby sit your pet, must less your child. You'd be unwise to give Nietzsche, Heidegger, Russell, Sartre, Gatari, Lacan the cat's can opener and house key.

[30] Western philosophy is the relentless expression of one grim straight man after another that leaves you desperate for a jest. Hegel, to his credit, can't suppress the rare joke ("Animals are not cut off from the wisdom of scorning physical things; without much ado, the gobble them up."), evidence for his humanity and system. Hegel, of all people, does not take himself *absolutely* seriously.

[31] When Adorno writes his nice adage "A splinter in your eye is the best magnifying glass," a proposition preposterous in fact and refutable as trope by the merest "no," he is being verbally indulgent in a way he never would have allowed poor, doomed Benjamin. Indeed, it sounds like what is hardly ever encountered – glib Benjamin.

[32] Every man looks back to the bowl to see how his bowel movement is doing. Ronald Reagan in his usual brown suit, warm, winking, familiar.

[33] *Notes on cancer.* The cure for cancer is buried in a WWI bone yard (the Deco ossuary at Verdun) or gone up in smoke at Auschwitz. The terrible wastage of minds must have terrible consequences.

It is reported that no one with heart disease succumbs of cancer. Nor do cancer patients die of heart disease.

Given that malignant cells have distinctive protein coats and irregular shapes, it would seem possible to train a piranha type parasite or T-cell to gobble them up.

Having exploited an entire continent, Americans proceeded to consume the majority of the world's resources and so it's entirely proper that every sprawling American city has a medical school with its pathological library of hideous, excised tumors; cancer being capitalism's definitely growing and consumptive totem.

[34] *Feminology.* Men who describe women as another race are contemptible, gross in the hubris in that they have so studied the species as to articulate, as they always do, their "Science of Woman."

[35] *Anthropology*. More than wealth, comforts, life and women — all of which they would sacrifice (and still hope to gain), men desire Victory. I am reminded of Gen. John Bell Hood, his arm shattered (Gettysburg), " a flesh wound"; his leg shot off (Chickamauga) "a mere scratch," the original of Monty Python's dismembered, feisty knight, who well might have said "Strap me to me to my horse boys, the less of me to hit, the more I am the man. And I have just begun to fight."

[36] Kings have a lot to answer for: foppery, foolery, abuse of power, arrogance, wars, corruption, extravagant waste, the massive slaughter of animals. But a single figure steps onstage and a voice rises, the music of Purcell. Are we answered?

[37] *The perfect inoculation*. In love, those that betray you confer great gifts in the act, the chiefest that they can never again *exactly* betray you. Such pure, inadvertent generosity should not be despised.

[38] The betrayed legitimately bewail that in a world where justice is very hit and miss, they have gotten exactly what they deserve.

[39] It's pathetic, old writers who after a lifetime of labor can't stop churning out the stuff no matter how repetitive or inferior compared to the produce of their high season. Decrepit poets are the worst, their later poems like bits of dehydrated fruit, tasteless, indistinguishable and chewy compared to the living pulp.

[40] After his stroke, the poet wrote not as well so that even though his achievement still stood, root and branch, it was as if all the leaves had suddenly dropped. There'd be no new growth and one missed being in his verdant shadow.

[41] The two most analyzed events in history: the Crucifixion and the assassination of JFK. In the case of Jesus, the perps are well known, Romans and High Priests. For JFK, it's a jostling myriad, the CIA, the KKK, Edger Hoover, the oilmen, the steel barons, the pro and anti Castro Cubans, the Mafiosi, the cold cocked husbands, the miracle being the competing bullets didn't deflect off one another so Kennedy survives. This decade and the last, an old geezer gasps out on his deathbed "Oswald was the patsy, I shot Kennedy." Disciples, all Judases, of Kennedy.†

[42] *Space race.* The great American peacetime achievement, the Moon shot. Nothing came of it aside from improvements in telemetry and navigation no one can name. A mere half century later few Americans believe it ever happened or care. Man on the moon? It's too distant and expensive for even macho tourism. People made do with Everest. By 2068, there'll be a flashy Chinese moon base, useless aside from looking down on the Yankees even as it is surrounded by our claimant artifacts: six left behind landing frames, the toy flags, two golf balls, the moon car and tracks.

[43] And so by the economic physics of some agrarian productive grid, every 30 miles a medium sized market town got prosperous enough to attempt its god-shot. The spires, Salisbury, Chartres, Cologne, aimed at the target deity, rising in perpetual liftoff. Inside, at the crossing, extra-terrestrial space, the cosmic wheel of the rose revolving and still. More beautiful than the best thing to come out of the moon landings that yet justified the expense, that photo of the luminescent Gaia stone, Earthrise set against a universal black.

[44] Moon Buggy. What was the point the Lunar Excursion Vehicle when, because of the chance of a breakdown, the astronauts could never drive further than walking distance from the lander? Faced with utter strangeness, American man needed the support of at least one of his two "best friends," the car or Fido and the mechanics of handling dog poop in zero gravity was beyond even NASA.†

[45] *For sale, slightly used.* Securely parked and presumptively in good working order, now, before they land, is the best time to sell the Chinese our moon coup.

[46] *Rationing.* On a good day, I may have one entertaining thought. I've know people who have ten an hour; at that rate they seem like nothing worth recording and so slower wits have a kind of "handicapped" advantage.

[47] *Fail Safe.* In that 1963 film, two cocktail party intellectuals discuss the aftermath of an atomic war. The dominant surviving groups, the prisoners and the accountants, will emerge from their concrete cells to battle for supremacy. The cons have the advantage of violence; the clerks, civilization and culture. Who wins?

By 2020, the combatants have changed; it's still the inmates (more numerous than ever), met now by the computer geek/gamesters. Both are steeped in violence, actual versus virtual. Allowed books, not computers, a few brainy convicts read whatever felons read, Falon, Sartre, Edgar Rice Burroughs and advance the tattered banner of culture.

[48] *In Concert.* The chorus is singing praise of angels when the real angels are the female violinists, lithe, focused, mortal. "And it came to pass the sons of god saw the daughters of men that they were fair and they took them wives of all which they choose."(Gen. 6.2). In other words, "Celestial studs want to meet friendly earth women." The O.T. is the mother lode of pornography.

[49] Something said or not and misunderstood. A friendship of decades over. The loss not only of continuance, suddenly one sees the whole relationship as thinner than one knew, perhaps ever a sufferance. The real loss – a hemorrhage of validity, the past bled white, nothing about the future or about the future only in so far as this weeping wound is the new "to be endured."

[50] *Tis the season.* The trussed up bodies of trees transported to the cities, there bedecked, gorgeously enrolled in the human symbolic order. After a dozen days, tossed out on the street.

[51] The desire for refinement ends up the love of nothingness.

[52] One symphonic work, embodying all "classical" music styles, plainsong to 12 tone, seems much easier to achieve than Joyce's attempt at something similar in literature. The obstacle is that composers are so comfortably competent they lack the rage for range.

[53] In reading accounts of the Great Pacific War, one perversely wants the Japanese to do better, admiring their tactical alacrity and unflinching courage. The warrior army that conquers Singapore should be unstoppable. But early on mistakes have been made; not bombing the fuel dumps at Pearl, not pressing the wobbly British out of a restive India, getting jumped by the adolescent Americans at Midway, flat footed at Guadalcanal, later, the one dimensional aggression at Imphal. It's as if all the hammering needed to temper Nippon's keenly cutting katana had beaten out a lot of brains.

[54] A mother's comfortings, a hunter's cries. Our natural bias towards the seriousness of speech is easily invested in the portfolio of brilliant talkers. Most human culture is (pace Derrida) the transcription of brilliant talk and most brilliant talk isn't worth much aside from its spell binding effects, itself a valuable cultural effect. Much hinges on the pivot of "most." Kant's elaborate rationalizations will assist scientists in their precise observations of complex phenomena. Hegel's morphological modeling inspires evolutionary theory and developmental biology. Human advances aren't linear, even at the rate of one step back for 2 steps forward. It's more like a dance, people jitterbugging off one another, mimicry and free forming motions, movement willy-nilly in various directions, with any ground covered on the darkling plain of our ignorance qualifying as knowledge. That's too positive; burning cats and witches contributed nothing to civilization. The point is human progress isn't straight forward, isn't predicative and in that sense is exactly like brilliant talk.

[55] If the alleviation of suffering is the highest human calling, the noblest human occupation, administering to the poorest and least powerful, is veterinarian.

[56] Every poem is guilty of the gravest crime – existence, its only possible expiation being the full confession and transcript of transgression, the poem itself.

[57] A species of intelligent TV sets, anatomizing itself, will conclude that its thoughts (images on the screen) are self-generated by its intricate internal circuitry. No need for a lonely human writer, actors, a studio of cameras, the broadcast signal. This is a kind of anti-materialist argument, facile as philosophy and no less dismissible that the work of former philosophy Big Men Ayer, Strawson and Ryle. Heidegger and Sartre would come under this criticism too except everyone knows they are writing philosophical fiction where characters like "Spirit" and "The Absolute" are described in a series of developmental adventures that have nothing to do with science or knowledge, their value a matter of consistency and compellance of narration. By this account, Hegel is a very good novelist and James, contriving his stupendously abstract figures of Maggie, Adam, Charlotte and the Prince, the most exacting of philosophers.

[58] *Rough magic, abjured.* Wagner had the right idea – the total work of Art composed of music, drama, and visual art. If the 19th century lacked the encompassing technique, we lack the vision and seriousness. Imagine a 21st century Golden Bowl, (Maggie, soprano, Charlotte alto, etc.), the baroque text simplified but intricately scored, the characters embodied via the highest quality computer programming and the "gaming" of the plot, formerly the sole privilege of the author, open now to any player via complex algorismic scenarios. The James Game, a best seller among the grad-student set. *Contrapuntal.* Millions derive pleasure and meaning from virtual reality in games and films. The chief limitation is that they are still *spectated*; once internalized and sensorialy enhanced, the adjectives "virtual" and "actual" can be eliminated ; ours will be a smorgasbord of *realities,* a brave new world where we do not merely view Prospero's Island but are upon it.

[59] Glancing at the constant influx of memos and proposals that come in my daily email, I am cheered by the thought that in twenty years none of it will matter and no one will care, not even the rat pack of archivists. It reminds me of the numerous ca. 1900 proposals for the Ideal City, all very intelligent and high minded (most unlike the daily email) made utterly irrelevant by the century's remorseless city shaper, the blundering automobile.

[60] *Reverse effect of care.* The beauty of Jefferson's Lawn; of course it needed to be preserved from competing contemporary erections. Strong architectural talents would not feel obliged to respect the great architectural amateur. Thus the University's fiscally straitened and defensive resort to building a series of 2nd rate Palladian sheds, white trim and columns added to your basic brick cube. The century's long result, a vast Disneyesque theme park, a pseudo-Palladian parody so facetiously repetitive it comically defaces the legitimate article. After Jefferson's, what is the most beautiful building? The Victorian chapel that's little, ordinary and stands apart from the phony facade of constructed conversation.

[61] People miss the point that Hamlet is a jerk; a spoiled, over-aged graduate student who can't ever resist the smart remark. It's only after his ego is deflated by his losing banter contest with the even better trash talking gravedigger that his self correction really begins ("It is I, Hamlet the Dane …") though Shakespeare, ever having it both ways, conjoins this pathos with the most bathetically comedic moment in his stage craft, Hamlet v. Laertes, mud wrestlers in Ophelia's grave.

[62] Hamlet, princeing around Wittenberg, is the kind of sport who'd kick a puppy out of his way and make a pun on "heeling" to the delight of his hounding pals, Rosencrantz and Guildenstern .†

[63] *Twelfth Night.* Count Orsino's desire for Viola is faux but aware his life is louche and superficial, there is nobility in his contriving a passion to acquire gravity and grief.

[64] Old people have no time for fiction, short stories and novels. That vague look they have indicates their preoccupation; rereading their own lives which seem increasingly fictional, with plots and characters little or nothing of their own devising.

[65] According to the Buddhists and Cabbalists, there is a higher mental project beyond daily toil and the toys of culture. That Buddhism is itself a cultural product, looking down on other ones, is fine; all culture is evaluative and receptively zero-sum. What's not clear is that your high lamas are superior to Bach and Shakespeare. Of course, if you can't be a Bach or Shakespeare, you are probably better off as a Buddhist, only on the basis of experience its not evident that your typical Mahayanist is better than the average student of Mozart or Cézanne. Nothing prohibits the best option, Buddhist Shakespeareans but it rarely occurs because the premises, destinations and satisfactions along the Way are different. Choices in such deep matters are difficult and always already made for you, a kind of karma.

[66] From the Mahabharata. "The earth is home to a vast number of animals, those we see and those we never see." A remarkable statement if it is predicting bacteria; even more remarkable if it isn't.

[67] Feminists are correct, the hilariously facetious fantasies of pornography have nothing to do with normal life. On the other hand, porn with its scripts, actors, directors, has the tenderest aspiration to Art, a teasing glimpse of Keats' Truth and Beauty. What really goes on between people in bedrooms is too high and too low for x-rated's clumsy catchments.

[68] Pornography always has a tired "been there" if not exactly "done that" aspect that is its most addictive satisfaction.

[69] Four decades driven by violent hormones – and no one died. A miracle shared by most people. When the banner of your flagging desire is hung up at last in the cathedral of cooling contemplation, be proud of the battle honors* but most proud of the motto stitched in the center, "Nemo necatus est." From middle age's position of declining sex drive, an anchorage of relative clarity and composure, it's easy to be smug; how wise one is, seeing how obsessed one was. This mature person forgets passion fuels perception and knowledge.

> "But love, first learned in a lady's eyes
> Lives not alone immured in the brain,
> But with the motion of all the elements
> Courses as swift as thought in every power,
> And gives to every power a double power …
> From womens' eyes this doctrine I derive,
> They sparkle still the right Promethean fire;
> They are the books, the arts, the academies
> That show, contain and nourish all the world …"
>
> (*Loves Labour's Lost,* IV, iii)

Brave words yet let us pity the young.

*(To the contrarian who objects to "battle honors" awarded to the selfish, hurtful and crazy acts associated with sex, the reply must be made, we are only human and in selfishness, destruction and deceit we often exhibit commendable courage.)

[70] He didn't have a single friend which fact he considered a blazon of integrity. For what are friends? Familiars you know how to lie to.

[71] I shared my poems with my friend, the specialist in Robert Lowell ; a week later he returned them with his verdict "crude." This was wounding since upon re-reading them, I saw it was true. Years later, I discovered Lowell's last poems are rough hewn, wanting to say something and not much caring how it's done, the definition of anti-poetry. No doubt my friend knew this but he wasn't going to extend to me the comparison, feeling that roughness has to be earned after you have exhausted yourself in finesse. So be it. The defense of my former friend rests.

[72] It is not hard to forgive transgressions; people do it everyday as a convenient personal and social courtesy. An offense of another order is when the same courtesy isn't extended to you. This seems unforgivable, any healing process is blocked and a chain reaction, toxic to both parties, begins.

[73] Since most people are uncomfortable with untruth, we suppose we can detect lies by strain in the voice, too many blinks, a looking away. Some persons are at home in falsehood and these, the great liars, are only betrayed by a natural air of ease and assurance, the signs among the multitude of truth.

[74] The only bad result of gay liberation: once upon a time, in the 1950s, a place distant as fairy land, the strong masculine woman and the sensitive feminine man were still enrolled as don't ask don't tell effectives in the forces of heterosexuality. Once they were free to form their own gay battalions, heterosexuality got a lot less attractive and interesting. Item: the hordes of women with childish features and infantile voices considered "hot babes" and the men who account them so.

[75] The important thing about Christianity was its congeniality (unlike Islam, Judaism and Buddhism) to expression by art and music. It had stories to tell and artists have always wanted subjects. The two needs, meeting, made the greatest aesthetic value producing machine in history.

[76] Like most religions, Christianity has a lot to answer for (crimes). Its best hope, falling to its knees in the court of mercy, is the testimony of Dante, Caravaggio and Bach who vouch for its service to the artistic community. The penalty is likely probation, the doctrine pardoned to irrelevancy which has already happened in civilized regions so that the value of Christianity in the 21st century is as an interpretive guide book to the museum of western culture although making this helpful observation in the United States insures you can never be elected to public office.

[78] *Heady brew.* Tibetan Buddhism: a compelling synthesis of alchemy, native religion and critical philosophy. The West, to match it, would have needed to confect its own mixture of alchemy, Christian imagery and German Idealism. The West's weakness, that it didn't; the West's strength – that it didn't and proceeded with the work of Science and Reason.

[79] Why so many sad thematics? Happiness comes with built-in coping mechanisms. Sad things require our grasp, an engagement of closeness and distancing that is an epistemic device of immense reach.†

[80] After meeting H., the foremost American teacher of Buddhism, finding him testy and full of himself, I mentioned it to one of his students who explained that high tantras require the augmentative supplementation of natural Ego in order to facilitate its subsequent destruction. He was, in her words, "suffering from a temporary therapeutic overdose of ego." Indeed, the condition is widespread. Who's writing these prescriptions?

[81] Conjoined with our animal egotism ("I want, I say, I am") is the almost correctional thought – "I am not worthy of the beauty of the world." To increase this alienation by augmenting earthly beauty, either by production or perception, is one exertion of a good life.

[82] T., the best known American teacher of Buddhism after H., said the suffering of Katrina victims was "explained by karma." This is less contentious than the American sannyasi who said the suffering of the Jews in WWII "was due to their karma." If all these remarks mean is that residents of the Ninth Ward lived in New Orleans and that Jews are Jewish, they are not objectionable. Neither are they in the slightest sense illuminating.

[83] The law professor was stabbed to death as she walked her dog near her home in the early winter evening. The place and timing of the attack was carefully planned, there was no robbery. Police believe the likely perpetrator was a manically furious student. Imagine him washing the blood off in strange elation and getting up the next morning for a normal day and all the days that followed, a respected member of the legal community, a family man who still feels what it was like, the thrust of the knife.

[84] *Drift.* The morning after the blizzard, quiet and then voices and all of them cheerful, even the man whose car didn't make it up the slope. He's delighted, his being stuck has conferred on him an importance his destination and arrival never could. Neighbors come out to help. Brotherhood of man. Children laugh, siding down the driveway. No school. The new world order. Good for one day.

[85] The entire immensity of the physical cosmos cannot conceive of the half an egg carton-sized brain that conceives of it. Naturally, this freakishly over organized bit of matter must be recycled back to the physical mean, inertness and death. So of course we posit a greater than physical matter, a supreme being who is like us and likes us and is inclined to preserve us in our mentalist oddity.

[86] God, they say, took six days to create the universe. The obvious flaws in the construction suggest He was a sub-contractor, doing a rushed job. As place holders to the inconceivable name of God's boss, we have Moira, Necessity, Fate, Luck.

[87] As philosophy students, we used to joke, "time and space were invented to insure everything wouldn't happen at one time and one place." This potential singularity was a god who has so successfully divested himself in creation he can't be found.

[88] Confronted with a completely superior mind, a mind better at everything than you are, your only options are to be become a follower or to revolt and rule in a subsidiary hell. Killing oneself, as Judas did, does not void the two options.

[89] As Shakespeare demonstrates so brilliantly in the characters of Benedict and Beatrice, a certain type of person devotedly criticizes the thing he most admires.

[90] A light mind travels further than a deep one which is limited to the depths.

[91] The third rate intellectual has traveled all over rather than abide in any one competency and like the superficial "seasoned tourist" is ever ready to share with you his comparisons and conclusions.

[92] Amundsen and Scott are racing each other to different destinations. Amundsen, arriving at the Pole, makes history; Scott at the Undiscovered Country becomes myth.

[93] The significant advances in life expectancy are due to lessening infant and childhood mortality via better sanitation, nutrition and vaccination, in that order. Factoring out childhood, the empire of medicine has added two years to your life expectancy. So the big news isn't what's on the front page but what's kept at the back, the obits. The world's foremost oncologist has just died of cancer. Yes, this death that was going to be beaten by pharmacology, cell biology, DNA/genetics and now, by quantum medicine, is still the leading cause of death. There is only one imperfect palliative: be kind while there is time.

[94] Youth faces death with an intensity equal to its desire to live. The aged fret but having lived and loved, theirs is a sense of having won the game even against the house's dark odds. Death, the next big thing, is not *such* a big deal. Children are sensitive to this, responding to what is more tensile than their parents' authority – the serenity of the gramps.

[95] Youth fears Death as the annihilation of the self. What maturity dreads is the loss of relation, i.e. when I die, sparrows, squirrels, Schumann, autumn leaves, everything I adore dies with me; the end of love. (And yet our births are common and vulgar, our deaths distinctive, individual and something to look forward to.) [h?]

[96] *Bonfire of the vanities.* One day with a 101 degree temperature

[97] There is a type of writer whose compositions will be much improved by the thought that each line he sets down *is* guaranteed to endure 500 years.

[98] Among the thousands of artillery rounds fired at the duty posts of a certain corporal in the WWI German army, not one even scratches him. It is enough to make one believe in a divine plan devised by arching shells that have determined no harm will come to the man so vital for their future proliferation.

[99] Not the least of Hitler's malfeasances is his rehabilitation of war ("The Good War") after the Great War had made the thing look bad. Killing to defeat ultimate evil (as it was) is right. And leaders are always ready now, post-1945, to designate the latest "ultimate evil" worthy of a good fight.

[100] We now are told that Pius the 12th was very worried about Europe's Jews, in particular those of Italy and Poland where the Church's intelligence network was excellent. So why didn't the Holy Father meet with the Fuhrer and attempt an exorcism? If one counters, an exorcist is a specialist, not a pope, surely the best exorcist could have been smuggled in as papal private secretary. From radio and films it was clear that if anyone was demon possessed, it was Adolph Hitler who as a baptized child came under the Church's cure and care. From a Catholic perspective this was a remedy worth trying, given the Pope's grave concern.

[101] *To the last magnum.* The German command at Stalingrad delayed the surrender of Sixth Army for several hours in order to finish off the last crate of headquarters Krug.

[102] General Paulus was right to refuse the Fuhrer's suggestion that he kill himself. Still, it doesn't seem correct that after a long but not inhumane captivity, he is released to enjoy a comfortable pension and apartment in Dresden when 95% of his surrendered soldiers died. The middle way would have been to set the capitulation in motion and take his chances on the firing line with an infantryman's Mauser.† Naturally, he chose the easier option of life. I'm reminded of the man who must choose between two women he deeply loves. The technically honorable action would be to reject both but heliotropically, he turns to the slightest advantage of love and life.

[103] To encounter Thucydides and see that what passed as history was shaped by drama, that Art best made sense (literarily manufacturing meaning) of the senseless acts of men, was an education in contradiction and the one thing I got out of university.

[104] Dickens' greatness I: the hearse horses at Talkinghorn's funeral, bobbing their heads, thinking "they die, they die."

[105] Dickens greatness II: Miss Flite's caged finches that in the ripeness of time she releases into the world: Hope, Joy, Youth, Peace, Rest, Life, Dust, Ashes, Waste, Want, Ruin, Despair, Madness, Death, Cunning, Folly, Words, Wigs, Sheepskin, Plunder, Precedent, Jargon, Gammon, Spinach.

[106] *Great War.* We've all seen the footage, troops marching off in too fast, reel time, festive armies waving from the trains, regiments fixing bayonets, the long guns firing, dirt-bursts, death-contorted horses, the penetrated ground. The documentary's rational narration – "The British attack to relieve pressure on Verdun" doesn't compute in the area of brain processing the images, it's history on parallel tracks, visions and facts, like the sex-excessed decades, ages 15-45, the violent clash of bodies run at fast forward speed, frantic advances, strange meetings and retreats, not a bad way to spread DNA around and even the childless can take satisfaction that the aim of the campaign is replacement. We are all bloody infantry in the war against death.

[107] *Pity the rich, for theirs is the Kingdom of Dearth.* We shouldn't envy the rich; if you work with money, you'll make money, it doesn't take a lot of brains or effort, just wade through financial meadows and the burrs of geld will stick. These gilded striders will pass a street beggar, his most important possession his plastic cup for coins, and ignore him, secure in their remove. Yet culturally, the moneyed are no less impoverished, a proposition proven when one is are exposed to their recreational productions, invariably stupid novels and clumsy art. In a sense they are worse off there being no "spare change of culture" or none they'd have the humility to accept.

[108] The dominance of Modernism and Abstraction in the 20th century obliterated whole schools of "realism," especially in sculpture, a harder craft with a more extenuated transmission than painting. It will be a hundred years before the sculptors of 2010, now radical realists, approach the technique of any 1880s stone carver. This one step back to one step forward qualifies as "vitality" in the arts.

[109] Certain types of second rate literature (Larkin's novels come to mind) and there many levels below that, are diminished by everything, plot, character, setting, occurring on the same wave length, consistency as suffocation.

[110] *HMS Aubade.* At Belfast, Larkin was proud of his rank, Sub-Librarian (superior to Assistant). Most appropriate entitlement. One sees a pale man separate from life and land by great depths of grey waters, a thick Hull, constrained movement in tight, pressurized, under oxygenated spaces, sequestered drinking. *Contrapuntal:* A man with three concurrent mistresses is hardly "separated from life and the lay of the land."

[111] Heaney and Hughes, in the best sense professional poets, were always respectful of Larkin's achievement. So what inspires his childish gibes against them? Something deep, something weak, something masterful, something small, the allure of contradiction that had women falling over like bowling pins before the bald-headed, four eyed Hunk of Hull.

[112] Everyone knows the most dangerously seductive pitchmen are not liars but the true believers in their product. Even as profound a person as Heaney must be sifted very finely when his topic is the subject of his livelihood and life, Poetry. Critics need to be very skeptical of all positive claims and mostly they aren't unless silence counts as severity.

[113] Minor American miracle, that Merrill who might have been so fluent and refined in interview and precisely poncy and precious in poetry, was the reverse.

[114] Merrill and Bishop, rare natural cats amidst the yelping hounds and sad puppies of American poetry.

[115] I recall when Eliot was the Parnassus of poets. One needed a professor or a guide book by one to reach the height of his literary references and how we all, serious climbers, made the hard ascent. Now after five decades of polyphonic post-modernist voices and The Pythons, it's impossible to read two lines by the arch-bellyacher and not break into giggles.

> "Thin patches in the seat of my pants,
> I pause on the stairs to pray and can't.
> Back at the YMCA, I cook steaks in my room,
> a coughing Cagliostro. Do I presume?"†

The only measure of a classic: a century of freshness and vitality.

[116] Those who criticize Durrell's Quartet as fiction for adolescents need to specify "very serious adolescents" to correctly lighten the put-down with praise.

[117] The worst thing that can be said of a work of art isn't that it's bad but that it's banal though there is nothing to stop another era from finding it "representative," interesting and revelatory.

[118] I do hope to have this little volume published – in Chinese. If only one hundredth of one percent of Chinese readers bought a copy ("Sunset glimmers from the Mysterious West"), I'd be a made man. Like so many business men, made by China.

[119] *Yet "Made in China" is always written in post-Hastings English.* Not one person in the cultivated courts of China and India even hears of the obscure skirmish, a few thousand barbarians knocking their brains out on the lea shore of an insignificant Northern island.†

[120] The Sino-American war is going to happen. The years before it already have the suspect smell of pre-1914 peace.

[121] Cut the economic jabber. 300 million educated workers can't compete with one billion. If it is asserted that some portion of the 300 million will specialize in innovation and high end products, some portion of the billion will also. There is never any significant comparative advantage for the smaller force except in a few economic micro climes, such as champagne and coo-coo clocks. When I was a child, the only imports from Asia were teas and tin-toned transistor radios. *Trenton made, the world paid.*

[122] However useful for projecting power on the imperial fringes, the aircraft carrier will be the victim, not the victor in the next great war, like the battleships of the 1930s that were statuesque, powerful in a sclerotic way, with ever more of their offensive potential devoted to self-defense. USS Ronald Reagan, named after the Alzheimered faux war hero, says it all.†

[123] *Midway is halfway to somewhere.* At Midway, when the Japanese were playing Go and the Americans chess, victory went to the fastest hand in a game of carrier attack slap jack. (The tenor is aloft on Handel's arpeggios; these are the five minutes the Zeros need to climb from the low level where they have smashed three hapless American attacks, to an altitude to confront the Dauntlesses, already turning over for their bombing runs. *Con l'ali di constanza* ends on a perfect diminuendo, we rise from our seats. Kaga, Akagi and Soryu are burning.)

[124] Great art, even at its most discursive, Richardson, Balzac, never tries to tell you precisely how to live. In Shakespeare, the one character that does is that figure of fun, former actor, phrase collector, and late minister of state, Polonius, (one of the Bard's tongue-in-cheek self-portraits). Philosophical and religious thinkers, even one so unworldly as Weil, are always telling you how to live. And so it's fair to ask whether they are good students of their own course and if the course was good – for them.

[125] It's impossible not to be impressed by Weil's thought as recorded in her notebooks. Insights, brilliant and deep, one after another. Only as you read, an uneasy feeling sets in – this is a person that isn't even remotely "normal," who can't support herself financially or even in such basics as eating and bathing. And if you can't do these things, you are impressing other people into servitude or you don't survive, in Weil's case, both. This is Holy Man's Syndrome; because I'm unworldly and have special insight, do unto me.

[126] In Weil's system, suffering, provided it is not so severe as to be annihilating, destroys the illusion of self-sufficient ego, and leads to what's essential, God (though she would deny this as too neat.) So what is the point of suffering in animals?

For Buddhists (Weil an imperfect Western variant), animals are individualizations of mind not yet engaged in correct understanding, actions and commitments, i.e. not yet Buddhists, their pain a function of their mental condition, as is Man's. All creatures are enrolled in the same system. This is neat. It explains why millions of animals are suffering – they aren't Buddhists. But we know why animals suffer, they want food and shelter and love, they live and lack care, they eat and are eaten. These are the causes of animal pain. As to being ignorant of Dharma, wouldn't it be a good for monks to read sutras aloud in animal shelters, slaughterhouses, to beasts in the fields? At the very least, it wouldn't be good for the monks?

[127] Because humans are complicit in their own misery, animal suffering is the greatest argument against a loving god. It's not enough that there be a canine heaven, that the dog doesn't recall his pain. The animal you see whimpering must never have suffered. Which is impossible except for Him for which all things are possible, including the impossible subversion of time. Despite sounding like a routine sermon line, the idea is high, attractive and one understands as if standing on the edge of a cliff why so many have gone over the edge.†

[128] Unless we posit a paradise for cows, pigs and chickens and all the little voles, this world is a terrible place where the only thing that matters is who eats and who is eaten.

[129] *Merchandise of Venice.* Shylock would not have parted with the ring given to him by his deceased wife (and stolen by his eloping daughter to purchase a trained ape at a party) for a "wilderness of monkeys." What is that wilderness? A vast natural order, a biosphere of thousands of acres where branches trash and monkeys howl, the alienable parlour of Venice, any society loud with jabbering simians. The wilderness of monkeys is the world.

Who is Portia, who has never suffered in her life, to tell us "the quality of mercy is not strained"? The quality of mercy is always strained otherwise it is mere generosity.

Contrapuntal. The quality of mercy, qua quality, can never be strained but Portia is correct in more than this technical sense. Mercy, appearing as naturally as the falling rain, should yet surprise the giver as much as receiver. Should and should not.†

[130] The Buddhists have a fine phrase for the mentality of our normal lives, "monkey mind."

[131] Quite correctly, Mozart never builds on the quick sands of seriousness, avoiding danger and depth.

[132] It is rare for any art form to surpass itself. In music, you can count the times one hand, oh yes, the Ode to Joy. Rarer, for cognoscenti, is the first movement of Schumann's D minor trio, when after the usual working out of motifs there's an improbable intake of musical breathe and the piano, strangely shy, tip toes to a place so rarified it cannot stay.

[133] Wittgenstein says Mendelssohn would have been a better composer if he had confronted demons. Mendelssohn's reply, "Wittgenstein would have been a better philosopher had he conferred with angels."

[134] World class orchestra, virtuosi soloists, this performance of the Triple Concerto perfectly realizes the composer's design, only lacking, because the musicians can't become less skilled and the listeners less knowing, that quality of difficulty and challenge integral to its composition and intended effect. Today it sounds beautiful and smug.

[135] *Crashendo.* Essential to the magnificence of Mahler's music is the sense, with all its rattles and shakes, that the freighted train of Western music is running off the rails. Strauss knows this too, viewing with regret the fatal swerve that Mahler foresees with a courageous glee appropriate to such a cacophonous wreck.

[136] The over-sophisticated critics must be right about capitalism being bad for you given the dominant thematic of popular music, the whine; whines about love, work, money, addiction, location, you name it. Are these whines serious or just another consumerist diversion? One thing's for sure, the sound barrier of whines about whining was broken a long time ago.

[137] The appeal of the British regimental march is that the basic folk melody ground, regularized into 4/4 time, with military band scoring, conveys an under tone of sadness as if admitting that a life of killing and being killed is an unfortunate way to earn a living. But the moral of the march, "soldier on" is nearly always a good one.

[138] Life seems very durable seeing that your enemy, surviving pin hole leaks in the arteries, the smallest virus and your own dark thoughts, lives year after year to make your days long with bitterness. It is curious how the recognition that you are someone's enemy gives so little consolation either in contemplation of your enemy's long life or your own short one.

[139] Regarding your weakest enemy, you needn't lift a finger; this flaw in the universe will shortly be rectified. That you are someone's pathetically low level foe mustn't detract from the beauty of this infallibly restorative process.

[140] The best way to disconsolate your enemy is to smile in his presence. This explains why every office has a cadre of hardcore grinners.

[141] Opponents count for nothing but acquiring an Enemy is a thing to be proud of. You've done something to deserve him even or especially if the only incitement is leading a useful life.

[142] The only thing worse than the bitter perception that those in control of the workplace are mean, narrow minded and incompetent is knowing that in their position you wouldn't be any better, that your virtue, as sufferant, is strictly situational.

[143] Anthropologists assert that the concept of progress is invalid and they should know. Curious how few abandon tenure to join the tribes.

[144] Roses have thorns, cats have claws. At the highest level, self-defense is integral to beauty; the woman who with a word or glance can inflict a wound.

[145] Amid the vast Christian universe of icons and holy referents – saints, disciples, martyrs, prophets, preachers, curious no honor is afforded the creature so indispensable to its foundation, Paul's tripping horse.

[146] After two thousand years of Christian instruction, it's not that hard to forgive those who trespass against us. We are not yet ready for a more intensive humility: asking the trespassers to forgive us.

[147] Why didn't Jesus continue his ministry after the resurrection instead of leaving us to the miseries of our history and coming back when he feels like it?

[148] One of those appointments that can't be refused though one had hoped and, perhaps, deserved better. There's little gain and no glory to be gotten out of Judea but new Procurator Pontius Pilatus is conscientiously determined to make the best of it.

[149] "Jews for Jesus" incites interest but only "Cats for Christ" would compel belief.

[150] Despite explaining to her that Islam is ailurophilic, that Mohammed himself cut off the sleeve of his robe rather than disturb a sleeping feline, my cat stays skeptical and agnostic.

[151] The O.T. is important as literature, history, folklore and myth. Ethically, it's inhumane and primitive. The N.T., dismissible as history, is ethically promising. This odd coupling of highly asymmetrical materials, like electrolytic metals, accounts for a great deal of The Book's interest.

[152] Benjamin's image is deservedly iconic, the Angel of History looks backward and what we see as the wind of progress, it sees as a storm of devastation. Yet I prefer Shakespeare's picture of little surrounded surfaces, our consciousness, the planet, the cosmos itself bounded by indifferent and eroding infinity, these "banks and shoals of time."

[153] Wise men can't agree. The Book of Living Well and The Book of Dying Serenely, is that one volume or two?

[154] *Utopia*. Inexhaustible energy, renewable drinking water and land, ample food, the distance is short but the road is jammed.

[155] Despite the vast human capacity for invention, the creative potential of capitalism, the world is beginning to look like a bright labeled product past its sell by date. *Despite?*

[156] Capitalism must expand to survive (Marx). Now that it is universal geographically (excepting the beleaguered fantasy states of Cuba and North Korea), it must more intensely commercialize the intimate and the natural; Segways say, instead of walking. The largest entrepreneurial continent is untouched. Brief, medically managed Near Death Experiences are just the beginning.

[157] It is easy to juggle concepts and spin abstractions in your own language. The one good test of any philosophy is how compelling it sounds in translation. Plato and Kant come out pretty well. One is reminded of the 1900 German student who read Hegel in one of the great Edwardian English versions and exclaimed, "Mein Gott, der Nebel ist gegangen." (Let us hope he was spared acquaintance with another example of English clarity, the ten shot, rapid firing Lee-Enfield rifle which young German soldiers mistranslated as "machine gun.")

[158] Anonymous TLS reviewer: "Austria never had the biggest army, the best lead or equipped but always, Austria had an army." Is this observation true, and why is it so curiously consoling? *Mediocrity, under duress, can exhibit a noble resiliency.*

[159] Decades after the conquest, the last Aztec warriors observed "your men were nothing, your horses, gods of courage."

[160] The Aztecs rip out the hearts of captives to keep the universe wound up. The Spanish burn heretics to keep God contented. Apart from the fate of ordinary Indians, one can take satisfaction in the contestation of these cruel imperial elites; never have enemies better deserved each other. And yet there is a space for sympathy, apprehending their first meeting on the causeway to Tenoticlan, the Spanish sick with desire seeing the natives so casually bedecked with gold, the Aztecs set to bestow on these dangerous strangers the thing they hold most precious – gleaming cloaks made from turquoise feathers of the shy, the forest dwelling quetzalqutal.†

[161] Who was more rational, the rapacious Spanish, retching from their visit to the blood encrusted temple, telling Montezuma he must accept Christ or that mild man replying "our gods have been good to us and we like them."

[162] The best argument against materialism – matter isn't material, the smallest quantum particles aren't things but forces, discovered and described by mathematics. It's all pretty mental. Of course, to say the material is immaterial is simply to redescribe the issues. Dust, rocks, cars are all then immaterial. We are left with the same problems. "Daddy, where's the Christmas tree?" "Christmas tree heaven, Johnny." "Where's grandpa? – the best answer (to keep it consistent) – "Christmas tree heaven."

[163] Sparrows see automobiles as shelter from sun in summer, snow in winter and as moving dangers. They can't conceive the real meaning of "car," theirs a knowing nexus of needs and hazards. Our knowledge of the universe, even with the laws of physics, isn't much better.

[164] If we live in Hope (and we do), the corollary is we die from knowing. We must face the facts, one of which is Pandora's ultimate: facts are the ground, burial and garden plot of Hope. So to the renaissance English meaning of "die"; an expiration, a consummation. The deepest fulfillment of hope is in coming, however hazardously, to knowledge. (Curious to think of a world without "facts" but the word comes into its common usage quite late. And the world is changing; as I type this I am also making love to a female simulacrum in the cyberberg "Sexperience." Is that a fact?)†

[165] The desire for life (action) and the desire for death (rest), these are the two opposing weights that keep us ballasted and upright upon this spinning globe.

[167] In Boston's 1840s neighborhoods where cars are banned from parking, it's like stepping into the 19th century, brick walks and buildings, boot scrapers on the granite stairs, horse posts, gaslights and iron grill work. These facts of endurance are cheering even if there's no sign of the crinoline skirted, frock-coated people.

[168] After just a day's rain, the Public Garden lagoon spills out into the walkways and every low lying corner is waterlogged as this locality aspires despite centuries of engineering to its preferred state of marsh and water meadow which only a optimist would doubt its likelihood of achieving.

[169] How often, feeling the wet wind and hearing the liquid sounds, it has seemed the solution to every human grief and folly was in the falling rain.

[170] We are not so much machines for remembering as mechanisms for forgetting. It is entirely proper that such devices are themselves discarded and forgotten.

[171] Viewing my life as a film, I've often thought the trailer of highlights was all anyone (including myself) needed to see.

[172] The first time your hear yourself on audio tape or see your self on video, you can't believe the rather odd, unattractive individual on display is actually you except by a mirror reflex of painful elimination – it's not anybody else. It's worth keeping in mind: this is how others see you. No wonder film and TV stars are so unbalanced, coming out the other end and having to consider themselves alluring.

[173] People have immense natural resistance to the recognition that they are detestable. This is as it should be; the despicably self-aware are dangerous.

[174] It is incorrect to think of Lear as Shakespeare's greatest tragedy. Tragedy always concerns the undermining of noble individuals, Hamlet or Othello, the latter superior to the former. No one should much care about the hale old fool with authority who becomes the weak old fool without any. The play happens in a wan light where all human values – affection, hierarchy, property and right are almost completely eclipsed. When they emerge again, if they do, our confidence in them is diluted. Shakespeare may have known that "Leer" is German for "empty"; King Lear, King Nothingness, (and "nothing" the most common evaluative noun in the play), a tragedy not of individuals but of essences and existence.

[175] Let's hope that Nabokov's patronizing attitude to Austen was due to mere prejudice – no women in his great writers club and not to what I fear was the case, a proud inability to recognize the subtlest of nuance in his adopted language.

[176] Too frequently, Nabokov and Joyce convey their pleasure with themselves, brilliance as smugness. They seem unaware (or don't care) that this is aesthetic effect, an aesthetic defect that makes them look small compared to the modest, anonymous "Man of Stratford" who, in a godlike way, never appears in his vast creation. Even the Sonnets, in all their intimacy are not so much autobiographical fragments as transcripts of a voice. Which is not to diminish Rowse's identification of the Dark Lady as a real person, one Emila Bossana, that must be correct given the sneering way his peers rejected it. Does it matter that Shakespeare's mistress was half Jewish? Probably not but Romantics would like to think that Shakespeare's remarkably sympathetic portrait of Shylock owes something to a relationship that however badly it ended instructed him in humanity.

[177] Wittgenstein's failing effort in the last decade of his life to appreciate Shakespeare is pathetic. The problem is not language (Wittgenstein's English was very good) but Shakespeare's ever variant heterogeneity. *Contrapuntal.* One senses that after a few lessons in basic logic, Shakespeare would have understood Wittgenstein very well until like a cat, he lost interest and walked away.

[178] Shakespeare's imagination is so strong he sees through all the vanities of imagination – religion, love, art. What he finally believes in is real estate, the Prospero of London theatre morphing into the prosperous landlord of Stratford.[h?]

[179] Describing kings with utter realism (a king is like everyone else except he dresses better and sleeps worse), Shakespeare did more to undermine monarchy than Robespierre.

[180] The presentation of cruelty is sometimes a meditation on mercy.

[181] Medicine continually invents new types of tortuous "cures" because profit lies in extended illness, not health or death.

[182] In response to your doctor's question, how much do you drink, usually posed in two parts, do you drink and how much, it's not good to reply "less than most doctors." Your doctor, who drinks, will appreciate the accuracy (less than three daily "units") but not the attitude.

[183] Having tested the proposition with several bouts of sobriety, the old man who drinks is convinced he's more interesting than the old man who doesn't.

[184] Elderly men are distinguished by their aromas; a slightly sweet scent indicates a mild man of generous disposition, a sour smell, a sour one. This dogma was disclosed to me by an old Tibetan monk who had been standing near the incense.

[185] I've yet to meet the young person who appreciates my mildness is due to intensities that cancel themselves out.

[186] Persons whose cats have recently died often see little scampering shadows, these ghosts no more than a trick of eye and brain. That is how we appear to objects – fast moving insubstancials. Only unlike the faux cat ghost, we possess will and force and every now and then break an object as if to show it who is boss. The object quickly reaches a point of material invulnerability: to the shards of the shattered vase you are once again a fleeting nonentity.

[187] From the perspective of age, it's clear that what was most real about one's Self was the quest to arrive at a reasonably comfortable personhood. Once there, it's no more real or less than one of those plausible sounding government spokesmen, mouthing the party line that's a rendition of all the conflicts and compromises that went on between obscurely numerous competing bureaus and departments.

[188] Philosophers such as Cioran who spent their entire lives espousing the virtue of suicide and die, as he did, of natural causes in their eighties are not so much contemptible as facetious. One thinks of Harold's house carls, sharpening bright axes before the long road to Stamford Bridge and Hastings, their credo "A man should not expire upon a bed of straw." Granted there is a difference between suicide and death in battle but not so great as between posturing and meaning what you say.

[189] *Cosmologies.* While the research is intricate, the discovery that the universe expands until it can't and then shrinks until it can't, is utterly banal, far less interesting than that of the old whiskey reeking man with nicotine stained fingers who works his handicapping charts to identity the 10 to 1 nag in the last race and wins $100 on the ten dollar bet. Which he reinvests in the booze and tobacco that are the helium and hydrogen of his personal cosmos.

Given an infinite universe, where personal identity is a *finite* arrangement of molecules, there are an infinite number of "Page Nelsons" writing this sentence, another infinite number that didn't dot the i of infinite and so forth. This is Nietzsche's "eternal return" always already actualized in space as an "endless repetition" (like a mirror image reflected in a mirror) that is morally and, more importantly, aesthetically repugnant.

If this is Science, I am driven to belief (there are no atheists in Black Holes) in the god of the Cabbalists who limited himself ("simsum"), contracting infinity to make a vast if finite universe containing a single "Page Nelson" who is technically unique, definitely temporary and one more than is required.

Universe A. Here, as we have been told by physicists for eighty years, nothing goes faster than the speed of light. *Universe B.* Here, particles, such as neutrinos, sometimes go faster than light. *Universe C.* In this universe, particles such as neutrinos, speedos and geisters routinely exceed 186,000 miles per second, doubling back via time travel and repeating the trip at the normative speed to preserve appearances. This seems to be the root universe of the other two. The only being that knows is Schrödinger's cat that sees much, says nothing and blinks.

[190] The disturbing thing about life isn't its brevity (in a life of normal span and social opportunity you can achieve all you need to) but its "temporality"; the entirety of people, places, projects, problems that meant so much at the time which from the lengthening track of your life seem like stations passed on an 'express-through' train, on every platform, your younger self thinking "my life is speeding by."

[191] Krishna in the guise of Shelly has pronounced the mantra. "the green dragon and golden snake like unimprisioned flames awake." As written, it is not quite correct. Sensing the mistake signifies the mantra is yours.

[192] There are 3 horses to Krishna's chariot of words, the syllables, the overt meaning and the secret, the beyond meaning.

[193] On a night flight, a light burns out on one of the cockpit dials. The indicator is still readable and the pilot, copilot and flight engineer continue their conversation … is it the fuse or the tiny light bulb, is there a replacement, can one pry off the dial cover or do you need to go into the console, how is this fixed on other models of aircraft, where are the fuses made, how much do they cost – a nickel the engineer says. The plane is on autopilot, just slightly descending at 30 feet a minute. After a half an hour of diverting chat, the mountain looms up, to late to react. The accident of our lives.

[194] We can hardly conceive of the ascendancy of pre-1914 Europe, a high-beauty based on wealth, nationalism, sexism and racism which was, presumptively, worth the lives of the upper class men who enjoyed it and overvalued at the price of one dead, drafted Dobbin.

[195] The causes, the motivations, the entire strange physics of the situation were entirely plausible until I left the dream, waking for the working day. And at the end of all waking days, what then?

[196] True, you don't have a real self, an enduring soul, but no god, Christ, Krishna, or Buddha has your perspective on the universe.

[197] Taking yourself seriously is a service best performed by others.

[198] Certain Japanese people desire American informality, some Americans Japanese mannerism. The ideal position, nowhere actual, is this situational aspiration. Likewise the case of the long term expat, a part of him always pining for the old country, who, after decades returns to find it not much to his liking. "Home" was located only in the yearning.

[199] To think on the elations of youth, the crucial points of victory and defeat (chiefly sexual) is to have a surge of vitality, of youthfulness. It was then that our lives were most musical and even the most decrepit conductor stands rejuvenated on the podium.

[200] The twenty year old bride and groom are looking at each other intensely, no smile. I remember how she filled him up visually, he didn't even think of the problems already apparent, issues with sex, his envy of her energy and intelligence. These were white water, shallows, nothing to the force taking them out to the depths, the irreconcilable, the inconsolable.

[201] In attempting to conceal the effect of your beauty, I most effectively communicated the effect of your beauty and knew I was doing so.

[202] Research libraries used to be run by academic also-rans, low achievement doctorates or grad school drop outs who yet respected the A-team and knew what the mission was about. Today, the head men and women are pure managers, administrators, computer technicians, and money monkeys not good enough for Big Biz. They are never seen in the book stacks. Is it any wonder they have doubts, amounting to personal insecurity, about the whole enterprise (support of humanistic research), why the only doctrine they unreservedly and uncritically endorse as if it were a self evident Absolute is "change" and that nothing more than the next sequent thing?

[203] Now that a presentable percentage of books have been put online, librarians are busy dumping books or sending them to distant random storage depositories to effect the empting out of libraries so they can be converted to student unions and info-arcades. It turns out that librarians aren't quiet, obsessed, introverted readers but normal friendly folks, the friendliest, congenial as customer service reps. And when the electronic pulse attack happens (one A-bomb exploded 300 miles above Kansas) or the not so freakish solar flare, or the global terrestrial magnetic field shifts and all the computers are fried, as we sit by the flickering fires of chaos, who should we thank for the new Dark Age?

[204] Every prison is full of men who have convinced themselves they never pulled the trigger or thrust the knife but who remember the exact words preceding the actions they never did. "You are a liar." "You are not a man." "Gimme that, slut." Our minds, attuned to language, are more retentive of hideous words than ugly deeds.

[205] I have no clear recollection of the occasions I've hurt other people yet I recall every instance of self-embarrassment. This suggests the angel to better action isn't guilt but shame.

[206] The naturalistic novel seems already the most artificial and hence fragile of constructs.

[207] "She made no circumstance of thus coming upon him, save in so far as the intelligence in her face could at any moment make a circumstance of almost anything. If when she moved off she looked like a huntress, she looked when she came nearer like his vision, not wholly correct, of a muse." Something about "intelligence" and "not wholly correct" makes this the hottest babe in literature.†

[208] It's all very well to say that mega-money for ball bouncing is the working out of market forces as people freely choose their entertainment. This ignores the deeper cultural shaping. We could have chosen to stage Chinese translation contests. Granted there are virtues displayed on the ball court, teamwork, physical dexterity, determination. And in the translation competition – focus, wit, intelligence. Which are the virtues you care to promote by over rich reward?

[209] *Coffee, $1.70 a cup. Gold, $1700 an ounce.* A currency is debased when it isn't worth the labor of picking the lowest denominated coin off the street.

[210] Over 30 million Americans pass more than trace amounts of methane daily, as flatulence. This immense energy resource needs to be harnessed, (the Hoover Dam of the 21st century), via accommodating receptacle seats at appropriately re-branded sporting venues, the Gasarena, the Bloat Dome, the Methane Bowl, Fart Park. [h?]

[211] More people revere Michael Jackson than even knew of Andrew, Stonewall, or Shirley. Soon, the great entertainer himself will be eclipsed by "Mikao Yatsun," the Mongolian electric mandolinist. The cultural object is ever more immediate. It can still arrest the carnival cruise of consciousness but the two aspects, Subject and Object, are increasingly in the same plane, a superficial one, where depth and the power to sink (and sink in) is being lost. Everything is surface, or flipped, everything is depth, amounting to the same thing, a deficit of dialogue, dialectic, dimension.

[212] If it were possible to make love to one's mother at the height of her physical attractiveness only at the price, upon consummation, of instant annihilation, what percentage of men would find this an enticing type of suicide?

[213] Before actual death, there's the little death of the day after the final time you have sex. No wonder our first action after we've gotten it together in the Bardo is to race down and join our parents in the act.

[214] *Fruit salad.* Any American colonel or lowest ranking brigadier has more medal ribbons than Eisenhower and MacArthur combined, running from the shoulder strap to breast pocket, under the lapels and off to the right side, for shields. The net effect of neat haircuts, smooth faces, tight jackets and all that bling is alluringly corporate-feminine. If, however, having served on staff was a ring in the nose, "distinguished service" (what we civilians call "showing up") a pin through the eyebrow, Ranger School a lip rivet, our officers would be so repulsive they could stare down the North Koreans. It's mean to be facetious in this manner but neither is it commendable to flaunt a resume on your chest.

[215] The retired ballplayer receives a Doctor of Humanities; he was a humane fellow. The successful business man gets a Doctor of Laws, his gains were mostly legal. The popular novelist is hooded Doctor of English Letters; she writes in English. The honorary doctorate isn't a doctorate because it's honorary and isn't an honor because it isn't a doctorate. What it is a sham and shams are shameful.

[216] The purest contempt is never contaminated by airing.

[217] You say some of these remarks are ungentle. True, I refuse to sit by the campfire of fellowship and sing songs about the Good, the Good, the good ole Good.

[218] The possessors of Kafka's manuscripts wish to sell them in a lot, by weight. To the reasonable mind that objects – wait a minute, there no such standard of value, the answer is that after the sale there will be. This will tremendously simplify the suspect business of evaluating literary remains. An archivist calls in from John Grisham's place. "Yep boss, we haven't weighed it all but it looks about 200 kilograms." "So that's about 22.5 kafkas worth?" "Right."

Now a kafka (two suitcases of paper) is a big unit, so there will need to be tenths of ks, "brods" and tenths of "brods," "roaches." For institutions that overpay for the heavy Grisham archive, there's compensatory savings on things like Jefferson letters, going at a mere half roach.†

[219] Sizing up the materials, cutting with and against the grain, planing down the knot, fitting and tightening, these are a craftsman's means to make the useful thing. In intellectual work, the theory, the book, the article is chiefly important as a means of producing craftsman like qualities of judgment and critical skill in the conceptual contriver. With artists, again, it is the object that matters. This is the evident and no doubt most facile distinction between intellectual and artistic labor.

[220] Flemish painting of the high period: exquisite technique making the real more than real, one is able to count the threads in the painted cloth, the spiritual made physical, angels in brocaded gowns, the Holy Spirit embodied as homunculus or dove, everything, even martyrdoms arranged with the imperturbable serenity and clarity of an organizational chart.

[221] Aside from experts and the retired, no one is reading the big novels Clarissa, Middlemarch. David Copperfield, Ulysses. As one "digitari" puts it, their *time invested / gratification ratio* is high / low compared to the web; such static texts could only flourish in an information poor society. And yet every month some exquisitely schooled young writer debuts with a 300 page novel, the idea being that size and contemporary scope will compel attention and not a bad one except so many have it. The future of non-screen play literature is small, already the multi-line aphorism seems too long. There's a market for perfect sentences but not many of them.

[222] The great literary innovators, James, Joyce, Beckett, by virtue of their originality are tough reading. Youth, with its high energy and good faith gets through them; adults mostly wont or wont ever again. So we have literary specialists, esteemed not for their dental type usefulness but for their curation of a value we respect and want nothing much to do with. For many professors, reading and teaching the modern masters is just a job and it shows especially to those that really care, the searching, adventurous young.

[223] The greatest enemy of the young and ingenious is the mature stands of conventional people who have flourished and grown fungoid like under mediocrity's dim illumination. Half of them know this, half only recognize mediocrity under what ever name is culturally current – realism, proportion, popular art, as a virtue. The combination of self interest and defense of the Good forms force so powerful that only one thing can defeat it, the incendiary flare of genius igniting boredom's dry, tenured wood.

[224] My attitude to art was flawed, fetishistic, the periods of intense commitment vitiated by never believing in the creative project wholesale; it was always less important than *[fill in the blank]*, like my orientation towards sex (bearing in mind that "sex" so expressed is an odd average of curious extremes), an involvement along certain positions (mental not physical), a matter of partialities in no sense wholesome.

[225] *Triple Interrogatory.* The appreciator desires that Art be beautiful and meaningful. Art anticipates her admirers will be worthy, while the artist, contriving the encounter, inquires "what are the stakes?" *High hopes, high Art, high risk.*

[226] Persons of a certain temperament create art of a certain temper though the relation is not linear/causal "A to B," but circular, spiraling through time, the work intensifying the type of mind. What matters is whether the spin is "rising" (Mendelssohn) or "descending" (Wagner).

[227] Young artists, we were all agreed, "art must give pleasure." There was no agreement that this pleasure had to be *pleasurable.*

[228] What should be the usual evaluative standard for any object – "would even one person miss this if it didn't exist" doesn't quite apply to art because new art creates utterly unanticipated conditions for its need.

[229] For men, it can be said that all cultural creation occurs in the moment before sexual consummation and all cultural enjoyment, after.

[230] Her beauty prematurely ruined by alcohol and heavy smoking, Virginia Woolf in her last photographs at age 54, has the haggard, haggish look of the soon to be diagnosed cancer patient. Given the state of treatments in 1940s England, a preemptive suicide was perhaps a mercy.

[231] While John Bayley's famous essay on Virginia Woolf is provocative, arguing that her ethereal personality had difficulty with the creation of vital "human" characters, he is also ungenerous, the insights offered as part of a larger project of put-down, his wife being a competing novelist of a very different character. It is hurtful to see someone so small strike at someone so great and emit sparks of truth.

[232] Once the mourners are inside the church or chapel, the funeral company's driver and attendants light-up and laugh. Given the nature of their business, this is entirely understandable and business is always good.

[233] One of the worst things about being poor is that the obsession with money puts one on the same level as the rich, only without the conveniences.

[234] The afternoon of July 1st 1863, Gen. Ewell doesn't push his corps up Cemetery Ridge, win the battle of Gettysburg and achieve Southern independence. "Why?"

"Sir, it was late in the day, my troops were dispersed, the Yankees digging in," all rational reasons when there were more and better for the advance. So what's Ewell's problem? Fatique? No lunch? Loss of aggression from his recent amputation and marriage? Or everything in his life, conception to that moment of decision. This we call Fate. And before that ? His parents meeting, extending back to all his ancestors, amoeba in the ancient seas, the immensity of genetic interactions over millions of years ending in "Baldy" Ewell at 6 PM on a hot Pennsylvania day.

[235] What eats at R.E. Lee after Appomattox isn't the worst that could happen – defeat, the destruction his homeland, the new social order of free Blacks. No, it's his successful hand in effecting the worst that did happen, the sacrifice of thousands of young men to prevent what wasn't the worst thing after all.

[236] However historically correct the uniforms, weapons and drills, one can't be an authentic re-enactor of Lee's army and be well nourished. Look at the period photographs; the only southern soldiers who aren't gaunt are the dead and bloated.

[237] *Greenpeace flag, quartered with Stars and Bars.* The great achievement of the small, audacious and ingenious Confederate Navy was the militarily insignificant eradication of the New England whaling fleet that saved the lives of thousands of cetaceans.

[238] There was a statue, a looking distant soldier with a musket, in the middle of the green two acres. We knew and did not know about the graves. And so that summer, we spread out our checkered picnic clothe, played tag, kicked a ball, sat and talked with the innocence and angst of youth ; who loved whom? Finally, the police took notice; we were expelled from our private paradise. Then it was certain, we'd frolicked over the unmarked bones of hundreds of young men who had died not on the battlefield but weeks later in pain at the university hospital. And feeling regret they were dead, contentment that we lived, it seemed ungenerous to think they would feel differently or take umbrage at our games.

[239] Riding the subway, it's easy to get annoyed at the various passengers, the kid in the rap hat, the punkster with her piercings, the three hundred pound man who if we are to credit his tee shirt is a sports supporter, the grim old reader. But everyone was conceived in the act (if not the actuality) of love and each of us is headed to the same destination we would not go.

[240] *Fake out.* I laugh at Death who destroys my body and spares my work, the bonehead going for the man when he should have gone for the ball.

[241] Given that we infuse ourselves with nicotine, caffeine, alcohols, all kinds of drugs and rich meats, is it any wonder we die? And given we die, isn't it entirely natural our appetite is for dangers and delights?

[242] If poetry in modern times has always been in a deplorable condition, the situation is worse now that the number of appreciators, the crucial assayers of gold amid the grit, are thin on the ground. This assumes most poets aren't readers, having better things to do. The intelligent reader of poetry is the rarest entity; their names circulate amid the poetry cliques in hushed tones ... "does she have an agent?" To a mature person of achievement such as a doctor, this is about as important as the condition of club sports. Where have all the good snooker players gone? Was the great era of rugby the 1960s? Yet the state of poetry because it defines the expressive capacity of language is more important than the health of the NFL, NASCAR and Professional Golf. It's just not as significant as the bond market.

[243] *Price Supports for Poetry.* The material threshold for poetry crafting is low, paper, pen; computer printing and word processing mean new titles number in the hundreds every month. Superior work is lost in the surplus. What's needed is a system similar to agricultural price support, poets paid not to publish. Full manuscripts would be siloed by the Ministry of Verse (UK), Dept. of Poetry (US) and the ploughmen get a nice fee. After a decade, the text could be released. I am confident most poets, readers at last, would opt for another decade of stipend even at a lower rate for reduced freshness.†

[244] The further language gets from the mundane ("the pot is hot"), the more false it becomes so that its highest realization, poetry, is, as Plato observed, all lies, its only manifest truth being a blatant mendacity. Alternatively it's mathematical, validity a matter of consistency and harmony (with possible external implications). The truest poetry is the most feigning; even so, one should not sign on to the proposition too quickly, like a young man eagerly joining the army confident his regiment is the best in the world when it hasn't fought a first rate foe in fifty years.

[245] The elaborate pre-flight check list, the intricate procedures for every takeoff, the hazardous forming into air borne groups, the hard work of flying a heavy machine and if all this is successful, the high probability reward of being shot to pieces over occupied Europe. Weekly the B-17s went up in their hundreds, piloted by normal men, a moral and physical image of such beauty one almost thanks the artistically inclined producer of the entire spectacle, Adolph Hitler.

[246] The basement of the Lubyanka, the penthouse of the Gestapo, the rusting Chilean warehouse, the deserted Irish farm, these lonely sour places where victim and sadistic interrogator collaborated in making the perfect condition and purest plea for angelic intervention.

[247] It's hard to admire a species that would truss up and face backwards the sick widow in an open cart so she could be more effectively spat at and reviled along the not short journey to her execution, a woman who had known luxury bereft of everything except a resistant courage that only further enraged the mob.†

[248] In middle summer the day arrives when the adult sparrows fly off and incessantly call to the fledglings that, at the nest's edge, must overcome their natural fear, find their natural courage and leap, fluttering, not flying to the ground. Then the parents come up, with cheeps of encouragement, a bit of bug, winging over to a nearby bush. This is a hard school but by September, superb flyers have been trained and just in time for winter's brutal winds.

[249] I have low tolerance for people who pepper their conversation with "like." The objection isn't grammatical, English being, well, tolerant. What the speaker is doing is making an even patter, a beat, a rap that's easy to perpetuate into one long monotonous utterance when the beauty of English, its challenging grace, is its differential velocities in taking slopes and curves, as if driving a responsive vehicle over variant tracks. It's the making like, even, that's moronic.

[250] Liberals and conservatives have different temperaments. The most determining political conversion occurs in the womb.

[251] If American century ended on 9/11/2001, the democratic pretence was up in 2000 when the Supreme Court stopped the Florida recount and appointed Bush. It's not that such dicta don't have the force of law, (we liberals appreciate that), it's that these decisions, such as Dred Scott, are not above reproach. If there was any cause worth police beatings and arrest, it was protesting the "election" of 2000. But we weren't going to be discomforted. We left that to the Iraqis, dying in their hundred thousands as all the while, with supreme imperial hubris and hypocrisy, we preached to them Democracy.

[252] Short Roman satire:

> Bush, son of Bush, our tongued-tied Augustus.
> There's blood for the muscles but none for the brain.
> Support our legions – Army, Navy, Air Force, Marines.

[253] *Non PC.* However deserving of apology and compensation, the Indian tribes that enjoyed tortures more exquisite than Torquemada's should not be romanticized.

Given the scale of Black Africans selling other Africans into slavery, one should not be astonished that had the power and economic factors been historically reversed, Blacks would have enslaved whites. Which is not to exculpate the white slavers but to vex the morally assured.

I have no hesitation in naming Shakespeare and [your favorite author here] the greatest writers, Bach-Beethoven the greatest composer, Da Vinci-Caravaggio the greatest artist, Newton-Einstein the greatest scientist and so forth. This ascendancy of white men has nothing to do with genetics and everything to do with geography and the accidents of history, especially the sudden death of Genghis Khan which achieved what no European army could, the rollback of the all conquering Horde.

[254] *Minor American terror.* How often I've awoken in the middle of the night, heard booming, could not tell if it was my heart, a not distant enough stereo or both and wanted whatever it was to stop.

[255] Certain persons are more alive at night. All their hopes and fears frolic in the dark.

[256] *Bad nights.* Mr. and Mrs. Mandelstam, indeed all the residents of the massive 1930s Moscow apartment building, are awoken at 3AM by the elevators running, clanging a little at each level. This is the hour the secret police calls and the not yet condemned count off, lest it be theirs, the tolling of the floors.

[257] KM books a few weeks at the cheap Mediterranean hotel. At night, she hears the man in the next room coughing and knows he hears her; condemned tuberculars.

[258] Biographers are usually sympathetic to their subjects so when KM's says "she was a liar," we take note. And if you knew from your youth that you were doomed, what would your relationship be to truth ?

[259] Reading KM's journals, a Benjamenic cat's basket of diary entries, letters, stories, the odd observation and financial reckoning, I'm struck she was struck as I was by these lines from All's Well That Ends Well "The weave of our life is of a mingled yarn, good and ill together; our virtues would be proud if our faults whipped them not; and our crimes would despair if they were not cherished by our virtues." That my new sympathy for her is uneffected by her being alive or dead or by my being so once these words are recorded is a limitation upon the annihilating power of Death.

[260] Dr Johnson v. Sir John. However well rounded, the rotundity of Johnson's pronouncements are tedious. What's lacking – hot wit from a combustive liver; Falstaff.

[261] Picasso v. Matisse. In old age, both show significant decline in quality of work yet Matisse never displays the auto-immune disorder most fatal to art, self-indulgence.

[262] Schumann v. Mozart. Schumann understands that sex is the substance, not merely a subject of Art. Mozart understands that sex is merely a subject, not the substance of Art.

[263] James v. Joyce. For all his sophistication, verbal complexity is for James a means to meaning. For late Joyce, verbal complexity *is* meaning, the difference between a book that radiates significance and one that conveys or more exactly, convoys it.

[264] *Dark Night of the Soul.* Matinee performance of Victoria's Salve Regina, 6 voices rising in perfect polyphony to the Queen of Heaven for remission of sin. How odd, the good composer appealing to a imaginary deity for a relief not required. But at night it seems clear, one's obsessions are sin, one's professions too, the little lies you tell and the little truths. Everything you do is sin: kicking the dog is sin, kicking the man that kicked the dog and not kicking him and slightest, most subtle sin of all, not kicking the dog. Your entire existence is sin so that your non-existence is a virtue except that too is a transgression and one you've came into life to redress.

[265] Until I experienced it, I did not believe a pain with no obvious physical co-efficient could be so intense one would commit any betrayal, from "Do it to Julia" to doing it with "Julia" if it meant keeping one step ahead of one's tormenting self.

[266] Cruel in concept but less in action, you presumed I'd never know I was the target of your contempt; pity had no purchase on the steep slope of my ignorance. Keenest angle of the plot – if and when I did know, I'd have to admire the thrust of the jest. The joke was more than on me; fitted so perfectly, it was me. So through time and space, the long maze of days, I'll be revenged on the pack of you. My reasons are compassionate; it isn't good that anyone should be so cruel and victorious.†

[267] People increasingly say "he/she passed away." We never say this about animals – Felix, Fido, Isis, died. This evasion is partly a courtesy, partly a keeping distant from contaminating contact with the carcass. Mostly, it's an avoidance of the way the dead have disappointed us by their utter physical failure. So we prefer "passed" with its sense too of having successfully taken an existential exam.

[268] Fish. Reading about all the dead U-Boat crews is enough to turn one off fish. But the ocean is immense and fish, they said, is good for one.

The little boy's goldfish never live longer than a month. Is it the chorine, the tablets that neutralize the chlorine, over or under feeding, changing the water too often or not often enough? What's certain: the fish mean no harm, want to live and die with great regularity.

[269] Mice. Those not too successful in killing mice will in time be rewarded with the acquaintance of extraordinary individuals, creatures of rare courage and intelligence. After that, you never can look at them the same way; the entire species has been elevated so that man who owns a cat has this justifiable vanity – the demonstration of his good intelligence in not underestimating mice.†

[270] Rats. Karl Kraus observes "it's bad when the rats leave the sinking ship but even worse when they rush to get on board." To which I would add "And even worse is when they hold a meeting, formulating goals and action items to proactively anticipate the challenges of a changing maritime environment."

[271] Kraus, whom I admire as the most skeptical and secular of men (Viennese Jewish, naturally), believed with kabbalistic fervor that error in language, either by ignorance or intent, accounts for a great deal of the world's evil. (Kraus was run over by a bicycle and never recovered.)

[272] *Dude, that's fucked.* Even if liable to elitist abuse, formality in language is based on distance and hence respect between persons. Drugs, poverty and abrasion in language are the main instigators of violent death in the United States.

[273] Silkworms in the five days of cocoon spinning must not be disturbed by any sudden loud sound that stops the intricate motions of their tiny heads. On the Spanish plains, at the first sound of distant rumblings, the people would gather in the silk barns with pots, drums and songs, making a resemblingly joyful din as the storm intensified so that even thunder was just a patch in the sonic weave, the worms protected by a cocoon of sound, the silver thread unbroken.

[274] After two weeks of Fall's searing clarity, how one longs for a more hospitable season – winter's short days and sight lines, the difference between a lover/stranger's total candor and a friend's congenial hypocrisy.

[275] The epitome of human made beauty and misery – the sailing ship.

[276] The arguments against a soul are so banally convincing, there's no point in repeating them. For a soul, two arguments of very weak force. The first Keats' (and not quite as he intended it) that the world is a great school for souls, some educative production occuring in a substance we can't define. The second, our life is a kind of dream and in a dream anything is possible.

[277] *Ergo sum*. A person is the sum of the information states of his systems and the sum of the sums, through time, a soul. Since time is an always extent and extensive dimension …

[278] That these jottings are of no conceivable interest to anyone is their one claim to interest.

[279] In the spring, the little boy plays in the alley on a heap of coal cinders dumped from the stove standing in the middle of the single room he shares with his widowed mother. A scene that is entirely Dickensian except it is the 1950s not the 1850s and I am that child.†

[280] Toys, games, shoes, clothes, paper, packaging, appliances, the freight cars of dead stuff following in the wake of my life make Marley's chains look like filigrees of grace when it might have all been different, the ideal of consciousness being the Dutch church interior (by Saenredam, Van Vliet) of structured space, white light and uplift. Even here, the reminder we are only animals; always, off to the side, a little piebald mutt is cock-legged, about to pee.

[281] *Void*. Forty years ago I did a kind of work that was repetitive yet demanded high attention. In the evenings afterwards. it was still present, a nothing, a void. Decades later I realize my sense of it hasn't diminished at all and, as if void (time passing etc.) transfused void, it is more real and enduring that anything else I did at that period. Every life has odd, "characterizing" features like this.

[282] It worth reminding that our lives are full of extraordinary events that only appear ordinary by repetition beginning with the incredible (for who can believe it?) spinning of the globe that gives us every 24 hours, glorious days and gorgeous nights

[283] Best advice for writers: poetry, feed the metaphor; prose, starve same.

[284] I never felt any pleasure completing a writing project, a negative reinforcement that functioned as quality control. As Wittgenstein said "in art it is usually better to do nothing than anything at all." Nonetheless, it was difficult to resist a drink from the last well of artistic if narcissistic inspiration, aspiring to write the type of book I enjoy reading.†

[285] Dennison famously observed, man is the most exquisite mechanism for converting fine wine to urine, a polite way of saying we change every delectable food into a consistent and stinking dross as all the while, with our passions, pastimes, works and loves, we scurry between deep earth and high heaven. The most fundamental question: why this something rather than nothing?

[286] Despite his chronically low grade dyspepsia, Edgar Lee Masters is justly prized for a few of his Spoon River transcripts, as when he records Jonathon Somer's debate club retort to Mr Tutt . "Before you reform the world, please answer the question of Pilate, what is Truth?" (Masters should have added, "And trust no one who answers the question.")

[287] Once one is no longer actively perusing objects in consciousness – love, sex, money, status, one can step back and study the thing itself. We grope for what underlines perceived reality. Certainly physiology, DNA and the laws of physics are correct answers as far as they go except they are also elements of the entire phenomenon we seek to explain. (Deeper, attempted solutions are "God" and the far better Buddhist 'mindfulness.') Meanwhile, we must lead our lives, helping others and being helped, taking time to cultivate a patient perceptiveness, "protestant" in its individuality that may yield if it hasn't already, illuminations of an answer.

[288] The name-dropping scribbler has the virtue of working *with* one of Nature's strong forces, the gravity of minimal effort.

[289] Charged with facetiousness, hypocrisy and worse of all, weakness, the flagrantly self-critical author has found flaws (ones he cannot or will not fix) that he faces by turning towards the reader, an awkward but aesthetically deliberate position.

[290] *Fable.* Adam and Eve, the first parents, feeling sadness that their children would live in a hard world, made up the story of paradise to give them the gift of hope. If there was a paradise behind us there might one be ahead.

[291] The regimental color with its scrolls of old battles; the book with its index of entries.

[292] Like that pledging sip of the sea one takes on the last day of vacation, our knowledge is a taste of hopeful brine

[293] There are events that give permanent shape to thought, one's brain is knocked into frame and events distant in past and future acquire relatedness and situation, as if one were looking at a map, this the place of a still rancoring defeat, that the site of a beautiful cathedral, everything positioned along longitudes and latitudes of meaning.

[294] Sickness is a grounding in truth since one's health, a precarious balance, is too complicated to be a durable reality.

[295] Once one has read enough to be comfortable seeing the trees and not the forest, History is revealed to contain more philosophy than Philosophy; every topic – identity, mind-body, ethics, epistemology tested in the only laboratory that matters, the world.

[296] Meeting him again after thirty years, I saw how Time had tailored all his idiosyncrasies to fit him, now more manikin than man, like a made to measure suit.

[297] Russian proverb. "if one has to go, one has to go!" said the sparrow as the cat dragged him away.

[298] "I am tired of my little stories, like birds bred in cages."†

[300] †

Metaphorisms

Advisory of recommended daily intake. No more than 4 per serving.

The aphorism is lexical junk food; the individual bits soon lose their distinctive flavor and one is left, surfeited and empty.

If poetry is taking dictation form the Muse, the aphorism is like those little notes one composes for oneself – "buy milk, pickup package, stop by wine shop" and the most important of all, "read notes."

A medium is debased not when bad work is mistaken for good, which happens frequently in periods of transition, but when no one can or cares to make the distinction. American poetry that honors Ashbery (style no content) and Levine (content, no style) is evidential. The aphorism is not debased because axiomatically it is a refuge from debasement. Many thoughts fail to reach aphoristic hermitage, those that do are perfect.

Riddle. How is the book of aphorisms like a small town race track? *The same old nags go round and round.*

The aphorist's big ambitions are fulfilled as small encapsulations of simples.

The aphorism tells one what to do in the dismissible voice of the insecure boaster who knows he has just one chance to impress. In other words, the aphorism has only a first exposure to earnestly speak, after which it becomes a mere transcript of literature and a low one, above fortune cookie scrollery, beneath book blurbiage.

Here lies the aphorism, an epitaph of thought.

The footnoted aphorism is my minute contribution to literary form.††

Aphorisms may by truth or beauty persuade or not. A subsequent interest lies in their apparently random arrangement, as iron filings find form from the force of a magnet beneath the paper's surface. At the very least, the words give lineation to the space between, a white if repetitive perfection.

Aphorisms are best arranged and read randomly. This is their sole formal beauty.

Whattage. More formal than the reflection, less formulaic than the proverb, the aphorism is a filament, a carrier of current between poles of Life and Judgment.

Aware of contradiction, and contradiction within contradiction, the aphorist doesn't attempt their resolution but their capture in a suspension so fine it is sometimes mistaken for a solution.

Aphorism one, two, three.

> "The aphorism – something I meant once." (Don Patterson)
>
> "The aphorism always involves a double look." (J. B. Stern)
>
> "Composed, read, and criticized, the true aphorism gains speed." (W. Ruminant)

The reflection or meditation is a *something* derived from a *nothing* (everyday experience); the aphorism is, in a different sense, a *nothing* (art object) originating from a *something* (thought, experience). That's about as Zen as it gets and it's Dr. J.B. Stern, not Roshi Suzuki.

You say the aphorist is anti-systematic. Indeed, that is his system.

The true aphorism is like a shy person at a party, all the talk makes it want to disappear.

Doctors should be subjected to their cures. *This is an example of the false aphorism – it simply isn't true.*

In every life there are events that make everything that follows "after the fact." *This is a facile aphorism.*

There are times when the statement "this work is deadening" is equivalent to "thanks for the morphine." *This is a faux aphorism, not exactly false or facile, it mimics the genuine article.*

The honest author flags all his pronouncements as false, facile or faux. *This statement is false, facile and faux.*

† Endnotes †

☞ [5] "Italy" would be the competing answer but according to the Italians, Italy has never been a nation.

☞ [11] Not that I doubt that high lamas return voluntarily and heroically, life after life, to this vale of tears to liberate Man from delusion, the most benign being that the progress of the planet depends on those who invent useful things (wheels, penicillin) or lead lives of quiet, undocumented virtue.

☞ [19] *Cavalli di San Marco.*

For six centuries they hauled that elaborate chariot, its glittering freight of history heavier each gold leafed year so that even in retirement, spot-lighted, roped off in the museum's stall, they still feel the heft and bite of harness, complaining with bellied, bronze neighs sounded below the tourists' murmurings. "Brother, I'm beginning to get mad." 'Me, I'm rather sad." "Well, this spectacle leaves me a bit confused." "Stay in step and don't give in." Far-sighted, they hardly notice the tide lines and swirls of people, pacing toward the finish they alone can see – Time's oblivion that's distant but (note their high hoofs) deepening.

☞ [41] *I cried when JFK was killed, when our charming, shinning knight was cut down by the shabby assassin. Now I see that grief as a period thing, a headline coeval with certain hats, hemlines, cars with fins. Now we know, pro and anti Castro Cubans, Texas oilmen, reptilian mafiosos, the CIA, the KKK, cold-cocked husbands, all were gunning for him that day and have told us why, with what good reasons. So many shots, so many Mannlicher-Carcanos… bathetic as a ballad, Kennedy's head explodes, at the center of every plot, Zapruder's rose. All dated, all fades. What stays forceful and strange is the ever spooling reel of doubt, a pale man between heavy deputies; a reporter pushes his question, a microphone's barrel – "Did you shoot the President?" Oswald's words rerun – "I'm the patsy, I'm the patsy."*

☞ [44] The point, that the car could make any number of trips along radii from the lander, isn't convincing.

☞ [62] It is perhaps worth noting that in the original detective story, R and G never speak to each other.

☞ [79] James remarks "it is the tragedies in life that arrest my attention more than other things and say more to my imagination."

☞ [102] Let it be recorded that von Hartmann and a few other general-officers did exactly this.

☞ [115] A parody of Prufrock.

☞ [119] *Afterwards.*

The next day, they took the woman to the place of bitterest fighting, to the bodies scattered like outbreaks of rock, clumped like storm slashed timber. It was hours before she found it, the scar blazing the twisted, hacked at leg. So they hefted him for burial, Herald, her bedmate and king, his face pulped in. The common Saxons stayed, grey or white in the cloud broken light. Ravens pecked at eyes and mouths, weapons were gathered. A few prisoners, roped and shivering, waited for their guards to point the way down the beaten slope, through the changing groves where leaves, bright blades, rasped and glinted, voiced the wind, strange tongues fluttering.

☞ [122] Naming ships after men is never the best idea because of the resulting linguistic oddity "We are proud of the Gerald Ford, *she's* the best ship in the fleet." What is unconscionable is having great warships named after dubious politicians when "Hornet" and "Yorktown," hero ships of the miraculous American victory at Midway, have no sailing continuance. (The formidable destroyers of the Imperial Japanese Navy ... First Snow, Fresh Rain, Cheery, Willow, Pear Blossom ...)

☞ [127] One is reminded of Kafka's great apothegm, "Only here is suffering really suffering, not in the sense that those who suffer are ennobled in some other place but in the sense that in another world what is called suffering here is, without change and without its opposite, joy." Beautiful, difficult to comprehend and like so much of Kafka (which preemptively redeems German's brutal defilement), mewing at the Tree of Knowledge.

☞ [129] The quantity of mercy is sometimes strained.

☞ [160] *Fates of Exchange.*

The soldiers, shifting in ranks to see the gifts, smiled but Cortes, ever courteous and grave, bowed low in acceptance, noting how easily the Indians wore gold – necklaces, arm bands, lip plugs that would buy estates in Spain, stables of stallions, a pale Infanta's bridal hand. The envoys, Montezuma's noble kinsman, were proud, seeing in what was laid down not submission but proof of power, their city bestowing such rarities, capes and cloaks, "shadows of the gods" they called them, made from "life-green, most green, what turns in the wind turquoise and emerald," feathers of the forest dweller, the shy quetzaltototl.

☞ [164] "Sexperience"™ is a proprietary, copyrighted trademark phrase belonging to Page Nelson; any use or reuse, including attachment to, adherence or impression on articles of clothing without the express written permission or license of the owner is expressly forbidden and all violations will be prosecuted with the full rigor of law, civil and criminal.

☞ [207] Charlotte Stant, as described in The Golden Bowl.

☞ [218] As more than one commentator has remarked, that Kafka's last manuscripts in private hands would be sold by weight is something Kafka could best appreciate despite his requesting that Brod destroy his papers.

☞ [243] It was Virginia Woolf who facetiously proposed a tax on overly proliferate authors.

☞ [247] Marie Antoinette briefly lost her sublime composure when she saw she would be transported in an open cart and not the closed coach that conveyed her husband.

25 Vendemaire An II

Hoarse from question and denunciation, the Tribunalists quietly flourished their verdict and sent the woman, bereft of husband, children and all Versailles's pretty things back to her bed of biting straw where in half-sleep's delirium, it seemed a brocaded servant stepped down a mirrored hall so that she must set her Age of Reason smile and take from his white fingered hand (light splitting at the barred window) the beribboned proclamation of the day – execution at noon. This she foresees almost contentedly, as if a last levee or audience royal but not the lurching ride in the open cart, the streets coiled into one vast animal, its multitude of mouths opening with a roar.

☞ [266] Malvolio's predictment. It is curious that none of Shakespeare's younger and gifted contemporaries (Jonson, Middleton et al.) compose the obvious sequel "The Steward's Revenge." A triumphant Malvolio was increasingly too political a figure.

☞ [269] The mouse that yodeled from the back of a chair, the one that quietly watched TV from the middle of the room, that dragged a bag of hard candy across the floor, the hero that from his "have a heart" trap prison, put his "hands" to the bars and stared me down.

☞ [279] However picturesque, such divulgences are always special pleadings to the effect "Because I am a self-made man, you should applaud the flaws in my construction." On the positive side, the little lad in the big man wanting a pat on the head evidences at least a conceit of self-improvement.

☞ [284] Or more precisely, my desire would be to write, in serviceable and suggestive English, a little book of truth. And what is "truth"? What you would give your life for after the Gift of lies. *Contrapuntal.* While the Anglo-Germanic entente cordial of "Gift" is a good one, the statement as a whole is portentous and overly solemn although it is possible the critical massing of such leaden objects could have anti-gravity effects.

☞ [299] Quoted from Katherine Mansfield's next to last posted letter.

☞ [300] It has been suggested that this proposition is consonant with the cabalistic position of Da'at. What would constitute proof of this isn't clear.†

†† My minute, original and certainly not unprecedented contribution to literary form.

Index

Adorno, Theodor, 31

Animals, 7, 25, 26, 55, 126, 128, 280

Architecture, 28, 59

Arts, artists, 108, 117, 219, 220, 225, 226, 227, 228

Aztecs, 159, 160, 161

Beethoven, 134

Benjamin, Walter, 31, 152

Boston (Mass.) 167, 168

Buddhism, 11. 12, 65, 78, 80, 82, 126, 130

Cancer, 33

Cats, 144, 149, 150

China, 118, 119, 120, 121

Christianity, 75, 76, 145, 146

Cioran, Bierce Sansrire, 188

Civil War (American), 234, 235, 237

Death, 93, 94, 95, 165, 239, 241, 267,

Dickens, Charles, 104, 105

Dreyfus, Alfred, 6

Durrell, Lawrence, 116

Enemies, 138, 139, 140, 141

Friendship, 37, 49, 70, 71

God, 85, 86, 87

Hastings, Battle of, 119, 188

Heaney, Seamus, 40, 111, 112

Hegel, W. F., 4, 30, 54

Hitler, 98, 99, 100, 245

Index, 291

James, Henry, 57, 58, 263

Jesus, 41, 147

Jews, 13, 100

Kafka, Franz, 218

Keats, John, 18, 67, 276

Kennedy, John Fitzgerald, 41

Kraus, Karl, 270, 271

Larkin, Phillip, 109, 110, 111

Lee, R. E., 235

Libraries, 202, 203

Mahler, Gustav, 135

Mansfield, Katherine, 257, 258, 259

Marie Antoinette, 247

Masters, Edgar Lee, 286

Mendelssohn, Felix, 133, 226

Merrill, James, 113, 114

Mice, 269

Midway, Battle of, 123

Mozart, 131, 262

Murdoch, Iris, 24, 231

Nabokov, Vladimir, 175,176

Nietzsche, 13,

Poets, Poetry, 17, 18, 39, 40, 56, 67,113, 114, 115, 242, 243, 244, 283

Pornography, 48, 67, 68

Protestants, 16, 287

Purcell, Henry, 36

Schumann, Robert, 132, 262

Sex, 67, 69, 106, 199, 224

Shakespeare, 61, 63, 89, 152, 174, 176, 177, 178, 179

Space race, 42, 43, 44, 45

Sparrows (and Finches), 9, 105, 163, 248, 298

Stalingrad, Battle of, 101, 102

Thucydides, 103

University of Virginia, Battle of, 60, 103

Venice, 19

Wagner, Richard, 58, 226

Weil, Simone, 124, 125, 126

Wittgenstein, Ludwig, 177, 284

Woolf, Virginia, 230, 231

Additional copies of this book
may be purchased online at
www.createspace.com/3741830
or through amazon.com
and other retailers.

www.ingramcontent.com/pod-product-compliance
Lightning Source LLC
Chambersburg PA
CBHW032137040426
42449CB00005B/290